Prayers
from the
Confessions

Saint Augustine

Prayers
from the
Confessions

New City Press
www.newcitypress.com

Published in the United States by New City Press
202 Comforter Blvd., Hyde Park, NY 12538
©2003 Augustinian Heritage Institute

Cover design by Nick Cianfarani
Cover picture: Saint Augustine in his study, Sandro Botticelli, Uffizi Gallery,
            Florence, Italy.

Library of Congress Cataloging-in-Publication Data:

Augustine, Saint, Bishop of Hippo.
   [Confessions. English. Selections]
   Prayers from The Confessions / Saint Augustine ; John E. Rotelle, ed[itor].
     p. cm.
   ISBN 1-56548-188-7
     1. Prayers. I. Rotelle, John E. II. Title.

   BR65.A6E5 2003
   242'.8--dc21   2003045881

2nd printing: April 2013

Printed in the United States of America

To
My Augustinian Brothers
of the
Province of Saint Thomas
(USA)

Contents

* * *

The *Confessions* of Saint Augustine is considered one of the masterpieces of the Western World. In addition to being acknowledged as a literary classic it is also praised for its religious content.

The *Confessions* is a prayer in itself, from the beginning of Book I to the ending of Book XIII. Augustine wrote this prayer to give praise and thanks to the all-powerful and all-knowing God for the many wonders manifested in his journey and for the providential designs in his life. Augustine remembers his past, reflects on the present, and puts his faith and hope in God's future plan for the remaining years of his life.

Augustine features all the beautiful elements found in the gospels and in the other New Testament writings. He sees himself as he was, searching for something or someone, dissatisfied with many facets of belief, going forward with the unknown, in the unknown. Augustine is the penitent person, the seeker of reconciliation and grace, the lost sheep, the doubting Thomas, the hesitant Peter. At the same time he soars like an eagle in the style of John the Evangelist and penetrates the inner meaning of the fourth gospel. He adopts as the texture of his prayers the words and themes of the Old and New Testaments. The psalms, the Song of Songs, Genesis, the Pauline letters are the single threads woven together to form his prayer or canticle of love.

In his *Confessions*, Augustine shows his passion for life, his thirst for God, his compassion towards his neighbor, and, above all, his love for humanity in God. Imbedded in these thirteen books are awesome, moving prayers, which depict the "everydayness" of human life. These are what I sought to collect in this book, knowing full well that perhaps some may have been overlooked.

However, no anthology of prayers, excerpts, or the like can take the place of reading the full dynamic work of *The Confessions*.

Besides the work itself I also recommend reading Sister Maria Boulding's enlightening introduction to her translation of *The Confessions* (New City Press, 1997); in it she provides a rich background for understanding this masterpiece.

Augustine's God

The basis of Augustine's religious thought is the triune God as brilliantly elaborated in his greatest theological work, *The Trinity*. It is this God whom Jesus revealed to the world and whom he manifested to humanity in his own person as God and human being. It is this same Jesus who gives us the Spirit of God which binds us together in love. Scholars place great emphasis on the christological thought of Augustine and rightly so. However, often Augustine speaks of Christ as head and body—the whole Christ (*Christus totus*) and not just the Christ of history or the Jesus of redemption and salvation. For Augustine Christ will always mean him as our head and us as his body, the two forming the whole Christ. These thoughts are emphatically preached in his sermons to the people, especially in his sermons on the psalms.

For Augustine the words of scripture, *Saul, Saul, why are you persecuting me?* clearly identify Christ with the Christian. The same can be said for the words, *Whatever you do to one of these, you do to me.* We must never lose sight of this christological teaching of Augustine, for it is important for a more profound understanding of his writings and sayings and, above all, of the prayer or prayers in his *Confessions*.

I close with this prayer of Saint Augustine, which I make my own for all of you who read and pray these prayers and for those to whom I dedicate this publication.

Let me seek you, Lord,
even while I am calling upon you,
and call upon you
even as I believe in you;
for to us you have indeed been preached.
My faith calls upon you, Lord,
this faith which is your gift to me,
which you have breathed into me
through the humanity of your Son
and the ministry of your preacher.
(*Confessions* I, 1, 1)

John E. Rotelle, O.S.A.

The entire book of *The Confessions* is one prayer,
Augustine speaking to God.
Yet it is timeless, and his prayer
can be ours too, today and for all time.
In this first section Augustine reflects on his youth.
As he looks back, he sees
the providential hand of God in his life.
We can say these prayers with the same realization.

Great are you, O Lord,
and exceedingly worthy of praise;
your power is immense,
and your wisdom beyond reckoning.
And so we humans,
who are a due part of your creation,
long to praise you—
we who carry our mortality about with us,
carry the evidence of our sin
and with it the proof that you thwart the proud.
Yet these humans,
due part of your creation as they are,
still do long to praise you.
You stir us so that praising you
may bring us joy,
because you have made us and drawn us to yourself,
and our heart is unquiet
until it rests in you.

(I, 1, 1)

Let me seek you, Lord,
even while I am calling upon you,
and call upon you
even as I believe in you;
for to us you have indeed been preached.
My faith calls upon you, Lord,
this faith which is your gift to me,
which you have breathed into me
through the humanity of your Son
and the ministry of your preacher.

(I, 1, 1)

What am I to you,
that you should command me to love you,
and grow angry with me if I do not,
and threaten me with enormous woes?
Is not the failure to love you
woe enough in itself?
Alas for me!
Through your own merciful dealings with me,
O Lord my God,
tell me what you are to me.
Say to my soul,
I am your salvation.
Say it so that I can hear it.
My heart is listening, Lord;
open the ears of my heart
and say to my soul,
I am your salvation.
Let me run toward this voice
and seize hold of you.
Do not hide your face from me:
let me die so that I may see it,
for not to see it would be death to me indeed.

(I, 5, 5)

You owe us nothing, yet you pay our debts

You are most high, O God, excellent, most powerful,
omnipotent, supremely merciful and supremely just,
most hidden yet intimately present,
infinitely beautiful and infinitely strong,
steadfast yet elusive,
unchanging yourself though you control
the change in all things,
never new, never old, renewing all things
yet wearing down the proud though they know it not;
ever active, ever at rest,
gathering while knowing no need,
supporting and filling and guarding,
creating and nurturing and perfecting,
seeking although you lack nothing.
You love without frenzy,
you are jealous yet secure,
you regret without sadness,
you grow angry yet remain tranquil,
you alter your works but never your plan;
you take back what you find
although you never lost it;
you are never in need
yet you rejoice in your gains,
never avaricious yet you demand profits.
You allow us to pay you more than you demand,
and so you become our debtor,
yet which of us possesses anything
that does not already belong to you?
You owe us nothing, yet you pay your debts;
you write off our debts to you,
yet you lose nothing thereby.   *(I, 4, 4)*

Ever-faithful God,
the house of my soul is too small
for you to enter:
make it more spacious by your coming.
It lies in ruins: rebuild it.
Some things are to be found there
which will offend your gaze;
I confess this to be so and know it well.
But who will clean my house?
To whom but yourself can I cry,
Cleanse me of my hidden sins, O Lord,
and for those incurred through others
pardon your servant?
I believe, and so I will speak.
You know everything, Lord.
Have I not laid my own transgressions bare
before you to my own condemnation, my God,
and have you not forgiven
the wickedness of my heart?
I do not argue my case against you,
for you are truth itself;
nor do I wish to deceive myself,
lest my iniquity be caught in its own lies.
No, I do not argue the case with you,
because *if you, Lord, keep the score of our iniquities,*
then who, Lord, can bear it?

(I, 5, 6)

I was welcomed by the tender care
your mercy provided for me,
for so I have been told by the parents
who gave me life according to the flesh,
those parents through whose begetting and bearing
you formed me within time,
although I do not remember it myself.
The comforts of human milk were waiting for me,
but my mother and my nurses
did not fill their own breasts;
rather you gave me an infant's nourishment
through them in accordance with your plan,
from the riches deeply hidden in creation.
You restrained me from craving
more than you provided,
and inspired in those who nurtured me
the will to give me what you were giving them,
for their love for me was patterned on your law,
and so they wanted to pass on to me
the overflowing gift they received from you.
It was a bounty for them,
and a bounty for me from them;
or, rather, not from them but only through them,
for in truth all good things are from you, O God.

(I, 6, 7)

Allow me to speak, my Holy One,
though I am but dust and ashes,
allow me to speak in your merciful presence,
for it is to your mercy that I address myself,
not to some man who would mock me.
Perhaps you too are laughing at me,
but still you will turn mercifully toward me;
for what is it that I am trying to say, Lord,
except that I do not know
whence I came into this life that is but a dying,
or rather, this dying state that leads to life?
I do not know where I came from.

(I, 6, 7)

Confess to you I will,
Lord of heaven and earth,
and praise you for my earliest days
and my infancy, which I do not remember.
You allow a person to infer by observing others
what his own beginnings were like;
we can learn much about ourselves
even from the reports of womenfolk.
Already I had existence and life,
and as my unspeaking stage drew to a close
I began to look for signs
whereby I might communicate my ideas to others.
Where could a living creature like this have come from,
if not from you, Lord?
Are any of us skillful enough to fashion ourselves?
Could there be some channel hollowed out
from some other source
through which existence and life
might flow to us, apart from yourself, Lord,
who create us?
You are supreme and you do not change,
and in you there is no "today" that passes.
Yet in you our "today" does pass,
inasmuch as all things exist in you,
and would have no means even of passing away
if you did not contain them.

(I, 6, 10)

Your will is that I should praise you,
O Lord my God,
who gave life and a body to that infant;
you will me to praise you
who equipped him with faculties,
built up his limbs,
and adorned him with a distinctive shape.
You implanted in him all the urges
proper to a living creature
to ensure his coherence and safety;
and now you command me
to praise you for those gifts,
and to confess to you and sing to your name,
O Most High,
because you are God, almighty and good,
and would be so
even if you had wrought no other works than these,
since none but yourself, the only God,
can bring them into existence.
From you derives all manner of being,
O God most beautiful,
who endow all things with their beautiful form
and by your governance direct them in their due order.

(I, 7, 12)

Set free those who do not call upon you

O Lord God,
you are the disposer and creator
of everything in nature,
but of our sins the disposer only;
and I did sin, Lord my God,
by disobeying the instructions
of my parents and teachers,
for I was later able to make good use
of the lessons my relatives wanted me to learn,
whatever may have been their intention
in so directing me.
I sinned because I disobeyed them
not in order to choose something more worthwhile,
but simply because I loved games.
I hankered to win myself glory in our contests,
and to have my ears tickled by tall stories
which only made them itch more hotly;
and all the while that same curiosity
more and more inflamed my eyes with lust
for the public shows
which are the games of grown-ups.
Look with mercy on these follies, Lord,
and set us free who already call upon you.
Set free those also who do not yet call upon you,
so that they may invoke you
and you may give them freedom.

(I, 10, 16)

You saw, Lord,
how one day in my boyhood
I was suddenly seized by stomach pains and,
as my fever mounted,
came near to death.
You saw, my God,
because even then you were guarding me,
with what distress and what faith
I earnestly begged to be baptized into your Christ,
who is my God and my Lord;
you saw how I pleaded with my loving kindly mother
and with the mother of us all, your Church.
She who had given me life according to the flesh
was very anxious,
because in her pure heart,
through her faith in you
and with a love still more tender,
she was bringing my eternal salvation to birth.

(I, 11, 17)

My God, I give thanks for your gift

In a living creature such as this
everything is wonderful and worthy of praise,
but all these things are gifts from you, my God.
I did not endow myself with them,
but they are good,
and together they make me what I am.
He who made me is good, and he is my good too;
rejoicing, I thank him for all those good gifts
which made me what I was, even as a boy.
In this lay my sin,
that not in him was I seeking pleasures,
distinctions and truth,
but in myself and the rest of his creatures,
and so I fell headlong into pains, confusions and errors.
But I give thanks to you,
my sweetness, my honor, my confidence;
to you, my God, I give thanks for your gifts.
Do you preserve them for me.
So will you preserve me too,
and what you have given me
will grow and reach perfection,
and I will be with you;
because this too is your gift to me—that I exist.

(I, 20, 31)

O Lord our God,
I give thanks to you,
the most perfect, most good creator
and ruler of the universe,
and I would still thank you
even if you had not willed me to live beyond boyhood.
Even then I existed,
I lived and I experienced;
I took good care to keep myself whole and sound
and so preserve the trace in me
of your profoundly mysterious unity,
from which I came.
By means of my inner sense
I coordinated my sensible impressions,
and in my little thoughts about little things
I delighted in truth.
I was unwilling to be deceived,
I had a lively memory,
I was being trained in the use of words,
I was comforted by friendship,
and I shrank from pain, groveling and ignorance.

(I, 20, 31)

I followed not the ways of God

When I turned away from you, the one God,
and pursued a multitude of things,
I went to pieces.
There was a time in adolescence
when I was afire to take my fill of hell.
I boldly thrust out rank, luxuriant growth
in various furtive love affairs;
my beauty wasted away and I rotted in your sight,
intent on pleasing myself
and winning favor in the eyes of men.
What was it that delighted me?
Only loving and being loved.
But there was no proper restraint,
as in the union of mind with mind,
where a bright boundary regulates friendship.
From the mud of my fleshly desires
and my erupting puberty belched out murky clouds
that obscured and darkened my heart
until I could not distinguish the calm light of love
from the fog of lust.
The two swirled about together and dragged me,
young and weak as I was,
over the cliffs of my desires,
and engulfed me in a whirlpool of sins.
Your anger had grown hot at my doings,
yet I did not know.
I was deafened
by that clanking chain of my mortal state
which was the punishment for my soul's pride,

and I was wandering away from you,
yet you let me go my way.
I was flung hither and thither,
I poured myself out,
frothed and floundered
in the tumultuous sea of my fornications;
and you were silent.
O my joy, how long I took to find you!

(II, 1, 1—2, 2)

I scorned your messenger, Monica, my mother

Do I dare to say that you were silent, my God,
when I was straying from you?
Were you really silent to me at that time?
Whose were the words spoken to me by my mother,
your faithful follower?
Were they not your words,
the song you were constantly singing into my ears?
None of it sank down to my heart
to induce me to act on it.
My mother urged me to keep clear of sin.
I remember in my inmost heart the intense earnestness
with which she cautioned me against this,
but these warnings seemed to me mere woman's talk,
which I would have blushed to heed.
In truth they came from you,
but I failed to realize that,
and assumed that you were silent
and she alone was talking.
By using her you were not silent to me at all;
and when I scorned her
I was scorning you.

(II, 3, 7)

Look upon my heart, O God,
look upon this heart of mine,
on which you took pity in its abysmal depths.
Enable my heart to tell you now
what it was seeking in the forbidden pleasures
which made me bad for no reason,
in which there was no motive for my malice
except malice.
The malice was loathsome, and I loved it.
I was in love with my own ruin,
in love with decay:
not with the thing for which I was falling into decay
but with decay itself,
for I was depraved in soul,
and I leapt down from your strong support
into destruction,
hungering not for some advantage
to be gained by the foul deed,
but for the foulness of it.

(II, 4, 9)

I sought the plaudits of other people

You were not silent to me at all, Lord;
and when I scorned Monica I was scorning you—
I, her son, the son of your handmaid,
I your servant!
But I was quite reckless;
I rushed on headlong in such blindness
that when I heard other youths of my own age
bragging about their immoralities
I was ashamed to be less depraved than they.
The more disgraceful their deeds,
the more credit they claimed;
and so I too became as lustful for the plaudits
as for the lechery itself.
What is more to be reviled than vile debauchery?
Afraid of being reviled I grew viler,
and when I had no indecent acts to admit
that could put me on a level
with these abandoned youths,
I pretended to obscenities I had not committed,
lest I might be thought less courageous
for being more innocent,
and be accounted cheaper for being more chaste.

(II, 3, 7)

O God of the created order,
the beautiful form of material things
attracts our eyes,
so we are drawn to gold, silver and the like.
We are powerfully influenced
by the feel of things agreeable to the touch;
and each of our other senses finds some quality
that appeals to it individually
in the variety of material objects.
There is the same appeal in worldly rank,
and the possibility it offers
of commanding and dominating other people:
this too holds its attraction,
and often provides an opportunity
for settling old scores.
We may seek all these things, O Lord,
but in seeking them
we must not deviate from your law.

(II, 5, 10)

The life we live here on earth,
O my Creator,
is open to temptation
by reason of a certain measure and harmony
between its own splendor
and all these beautiful things of low degree.
The friendship which draws human beings together
in a tender bond is sweet to us
because out of many minds
it forges a unity.
Sin gains entrance through these
and similar good things
when we turn to them with immoderate desire,
since they are the lowest kind of goods
and we thereby turn away from the better and higher:
from you yourself, O Lord our God,
and your truth and your law.
These lowest goods hold delights for us indeed,
but no such delights as does my God,
who made all things;
for in him the just man finds delight,
and for upright souls he himself is joy.

(II, 5, 10)

In vice there lurks a counterfeit beauty:
pride, for instance—even pride apes sublimity,
whereas you are the only God,
most high above all things.
As for ambition,
what does it crave but honors and glory,
while you are worthy of honor beyond all others,
and eternally glorious.
The ferocity of powerful men aims to inspire fear;
but who is to be feared except the one God?
Can anything be snatched from his power
or withdrawn from it—
when or where or whither or by whom?
Flirtatiousness aims to arouse love
by its charming wiles,
but nothing can hold more charm
than your charity,
nor could anything be loved to greater profit
than your truth,
which outshines all else in its luminous beauty.
Curiosity poses as pursuit of knowledge,
whereas you know everything to a supreme degree.
Even ignorance or stupidity masquerades
as simplicity and innocence,
but nothing that exists is simpler than yourself;
and what could be more innocent than you,
who leave the wicked to be hounded by their own sins?
Sloth pretends to aspire to rest,
but what sure rest is there save the Lord?

Lush living likes to be taken for contented abundance,
but you are the full and inexhaustible store
of a sweetness that never grows stale.
Extravagance is a bogus generosity,
but you are the infinitely wealthy giver
of all good things.
Avarice strives to amass possessions,
but you own everything.
Envy is contentious over rank accorded to another,
but what ranks higher than you?
Anger seeks revenge,
but who ever exacts revenge
with greater justice than yourself?
Timidity dreads any unforeseen or sudden threat
to the things it loves,
and takes precautions for their safety,
but is anything sudden or unforeseen to you?
Who can separate what you love from you?
Where is ultimate security to be found, except with you?
Sadness pines at the loss of the good things
with which greed took its pleasure,
because it wants to be like you,
from whom nothing can be taken away.

(II, 6, 13)

Let me love you, Lord,
and give thanks to you
and confess to your name,
because you have forgiven
my grave sins and wicked deeds.
By your sheer grace and mercy
you melted my sins away like ice.
To your grace also do I ascribe
whatever sins I did not commit,
for what would I not have been capable of,
I who could be enamored even of a wanton crime
I acknowledge that you have forgiven me everything,
both the sins I willfully committed
by following my own will,
and those I avoided through your guidance.

(II, 7, 15)

I slid away from you, my God

O justice and innocence, fair and lovely,
it is on you that I want to gaze
with eyes that see purely
and find satiety in never being sated.
With you is rest and tranquil life.
Whoever enters into you enters the joy of his Lord;
there he will fear nothing
and find his own supreme good in God
who is supreme goodness.
I slid away from you and wandered away, my God;
far from your steadfastness
I strayed in adolescence,
and I became to myself a land of famine.

(II, 10, 18)

My inner famine

I was not yet in love,
but I was enamored with the idea of love,
and so deep within me was my need
that I hated myself for the sluggishness of my desires.
In love with loving,
I was casting about for something to love;
the security of a way of life
free from pitfalls seemed abhorrent to me,
because I was inwardly starved of that food
which is yourself, O my God.
Yet this inner famine
created no pangs of hunger in me.
I had no desire for the food
that does not perish,
not because I had my fill of it,
but because the more empty I was,
the more I turned from it in revulsion.
My soul's health was consequently poor.
It was covered with sores
and flung itself out of doors,
longing to soothe its misery
by rubbing against sensible things;
yet these were soulless,
and so could not be truly loved.

(III, 1, 1)

The name of Christ captivated me

You know, O light of my heart,
and one only
that brought me joy in the exhortation to wisdom:
that by its call I was aroused and kindled
and set on fire
to love and seek
and capture and hold fast
and strongly cling
not to this or that school,
but to wisdom itself,
whatever it might be.
Only one consideration checked me
in my ardent enthusiasm:
that the name of Christ did not occur there.
Through your mercy, Lord,
my tender little heart had drunk in that name,
the name of my Savior and your Son,
with my mother's milk,
and in my deepest heart I still held on to it.
No writing from which that name was missing,
even if learned,
of literary elegance and truthful,
could ever captivate me completely.

(III, 4, 8)

Far above me your faithful mercy was hovering.
How great were the sins
on which I spent all my strength,
as I followed my impious curiosity!
It led me to abandon you
and plunge into treacherous abysses,
into depths of unbelief
and a delusive allegiance to demons,
to whom I was offering my evil deeds in sacrifice.
And in all these sins your scourges beat upon me.
Even within the walls of your church,
during the celebration of your sacred mysteries,
I once made bold to indulge in carnal desire and conduct
that could yield only a harvest of death;
and for this you struck me with severe punishments,
though none that matched my guilt.
O my God, you were immensely merciful to me,
and were my refuge from the terrible dangers
amid which I wandered, head held high.
I withdrew further and further from you,
loving my own ways and not yours,
relishing the freedom of a runaway slave.

(III, 3, 5)

In this section of prayers
Augustine looks back at his mother,
his son, and all those people who shaped his life,
and gives thanks and praise for the role
which they played in his life.
He realized that through them
the hand of God once again found him.
We too are shaped by those
who travel with us on our journey.

Look upon my heart, O my God,
look deep within it.
See, O my hope,
who cleanse me from the uncleanness of such affections,
who draw my eyes to yourself
and pull my feet free from the snare,
see that this is indeed what I remember.
I was amazed that other mortals went on living
when he was dead
whom I had loved as though he would never die,
and still more amazed that I could go on living myself
when he was dead—I, who had been
like another self to him.
It was well said that a friend is half one's own soul.
I felt that my soul and his
had been but one soul in two bodies,
and I shrank from life with loathing
because I could not bear to be only half alive;
and perhaps I was so afraid of death
because I did not want the whole of him to die,
whom I had loved so dearly.

(IV, 6, 11)

You heard my mother's tears

You stretched out your hand from on high
and pulled my soul out of these murky depths
because my mother, who was faithful to you,
was weeping for me more bitterly
than ever mothers wept
for the bodily death of their children.
In her faith
and in the spiritual discernment
she possessed by your gift
she regarded me as dead;
and you heard her, O Lord,
you heard her
and did not scorn those tears of hers
which gushed forth
and watered the ground beneath her eyes
wherever she prayed.

(III, 11, 19)

The loss of a friend

Woe to the madness
which thinks to cherish human beings
as though more than human!
How foolish the human heart
that anguishes without restraint over human ills
as I did then!
Feverishly I thrashed about,
sighed, wept and was troubled,
and there was no repose for me, nor any counsel.
Within me I was carrying a tattered, bleeding soul
that did not want me to carry it,
yet I could find no place to lay it down.
Not in pleasant countryside did it find rest,
nor in shows and songs,
nor in sweet-scented gardens,
nor in elaborate feasts,
nor in the pleasures of couch or bed,
nor even in books and incantations.
All things loured at me, even daylight itself,
and everything that was not what he was
seemed to me offensive and hateful,
except for mourning and tears,
in which alone I found some slight relief.
Whenever my soul was drawn away from this,
it burdened me with a great load of misery.
I should have lifted it up to you, Lord, to be healed,
but I was neither willing nor able to do so,
especially because when I thought about you
you did not seem to be anything solid or firm.

(IV, 7, 12)

There were joys to be found in their company
which still more powerfully captivated my mind—
the charms of talking and laughing together
and kindly giving way to each other's wishes,
reading elegantly written books together,
sharing jokes and delighting to honor one another,
disagreeing occasionally but without rancor,
as a person might disagree with himself,
and lending piquancy by that rare disagreement
to our much more frequent accord.
We would teach and learn from each other,
sadly missing any who were absent
and blithely welcoming them when they returned.
Such signs of friendship sprang from the hearts of friends
who loved and knew their love returned,
signs to be read in smiles, words, glances
and a thousand gracious gestures.
So were sparks kindled
and our minds were fused inseparably,
out of many becoming one.
This is what we esteem in our friends,
and so highly do we esteem it
that our conscience feels guilt
if we fail to love someone who responds to us with love,
or do not return the love of one who offers love to us,
and this without seeking
any bodily gratification from the other
save signs of his goodwill.

(IV, 8, 13)

My friend, Alypius

You, Lord, guide the courses of all your creatures,
and you had not forgotten this man
who one day would be set over your children
as dispenser of your mysteries.
You brought about his correction through my agency,
but without my knowledge,
so that it might be clearly recognized as your work.

(VI, 7, 12)

The love of a mother

My mother persevered in praying for me;
she was far away,
but you are present everywhere,
so you heard her in that land where she was,
and took pity on me where I was.
I can find no words to express
how intensely she loved me:
with far more anxious solicitude
did she give birth to me in the spirit
than ever she had in the flesh.

(V, 9, 16)

You, God, are never lost to us

Blessed is he who loves you,
and loves his friend in you
and his enemy for your sake.
He alone loses no one dear to him,
to whom all are dear
in the One who is never lost.
And who is this but our God,
the God who made heaven and earth and fills them,
because it was by filling them that he made them?
No one loses you unless he tries to get rid of you,
and if he does try to do that,
where can he go,
whither does he flee,
but from you in your tranquillity
to you in your anger?
Does he not encounter your law everywhere,
in his own punishment?
Your law is truth,
as you yourself are truth.

(IV, 9, 14)

Now Augustine reflects on the "God within"—
the God who was always with him
but whom he did not fully recognize.
He thanks God for guiding him in this way.
We too need to trust God who is in us.

Be not vain, my soul,
and take care that the ear of your heart
be not deafened by the din of your vanity.
You too must listen to the selfsame Word
who calls you back,
and there find a place of imperturbable quiet,
where love is never forsaken
unless it chooses to forsake.
See, those things go their way
that others may succeed them,
and that a whole may exist comprised of all its parts,
though a lowly whole indeed.
"But I," says the Word of God,
"shall I depart to any place?"
Fix your dwelling there, my soul,
lay up there for safe-keeping
whatever you have thence received,
if only because you are weary of deceits.
Entrust to Truth whatever of truth is in you,
and you will lose nothing;
your rotten flesh will flower anew,
all your diseases will be healed,
all your labile elements will be restored
and bound fast to you;
they will not drag you with them in their own collapse,
but will stand firm with you and abide,
binding you to the ever-stable, abiding God.

(IV, 11, 16)

Let us love him,
for he made these things and he is not far off,
for he did not make them and then go away:
they are from him but also in him.
You know where he is,
because you know where truth tastes sweet.
He is most intimately present to the human heart,
but the heart has strayed from him.
Return to your heart, then, you wrongdoers,
and hold fast to him who made you.
Stand with him and you will stand firm,
rest in him and you will find peace.
Where are you going, along your rough paths?
Tell me, where are you going?
The good which you love derives from him,
and insofar as it is referred to him
it is truly good and sweet,
but anything that comes from him will justly turn bitter
if it is unjustly loved by people who forsake him.
Why persist in walking difficult and toilsome paths?
There is no repose where you are seeking it.
Search as you like, it is not where you are looking.
You are seeking a happy life in the realm of death,
and it will not be found there.
How could life be happy,
where there is no life at all?

(IV, 12, 18)

He who is our very life came down
and took our death upon himself.
He slew our death by his abundant life
and summoned us in a voice of thunder
to return to him in his hidden place,
that place from which he set out to come to us
when first he entered the Virgin's womb.
There a human creature, mortal flesh,
was wedded to him
that it might not remain mortal for ever;
and from there he came forth like a bridegroom
from his nuptial chamber,
leaping with joy like a giant to run his course.
Impatient of delay he ran,
shouting by his words, his deeds, his death and his life,
his descent to hell and his ascension to heaven,
shouting his demand that we return to him.
Then he withdrew from our sight,
so that we might return to our own hearts
and find him there.
He withdrew, yet look, here he is.
It was not his will to remain with us,
yet he has not abandoned us either.

(IV, 12, 19)

You carry us, Lord

O Lord our God,
grant us to trust in your overshadowing wings:
protect us beneath them and bear us up.
You will carry us as little children,
and even to our grey-headed age you will carry us still.
When you are our strong security, that is strength indeed,
but when our security is in ourselves, that is but weakness.
Our good abides ever in your keeping,
but in diverting our steps from you we have grown perverse.
Let us turn back to you at last, Lord,
that we be not overturned.
Unspoilt, our good abides with you,
for you are yourself our good.
We need not fear to find no home again
because we have fallen away from it;
while we are absent our home falls not to ruins,
for our home is your eternity.

(IV, 16, 31)

Let my soul give you glory

Allow my soul to give you glory
that it may love you the more,
and let it confess to you your own merciful dealings,
that it may give you glory.
Your whole creation never wearies of praising you,
never falls silent;
never a breath from the mouth of one who turns to you
but gives you glory,
never is praise lacking
from the universe of living creatures and corporeal beings
as they laud you through the mouths
of those who contemplate them.
Supported by these things you have made
let the human soul rise above its weariness
and pass through these creatures to you,
who have made them so wonderfully.
There it will find refreshment,
there is its true strength.

(V, 1, 1)

A person who confesses to you, Lord,
is not informing you about what goes on within him,
for a closed heart does not shut you out,
nor is your hand pushed away by human obduracy;
you melt it when you choose,
whether by showing mercy
or by enforcing your claim,
and from your fiery heat
no one can hide.

(V, 1, 1)

And what of myself:
where was I as I sought you?
You were straight ahead of me,
but I had roamed away from myself
and could not find even myself,
let alone you!

(V, 2, 2)

Let them turn back, and seek you,
for you do not forsake your creation
as they have forsaken their creator.
Let them only turn back,
see! there you are in their hearts,
in the hearts of all those who confess to you,
who fling themselves into your arms
and weep against your breast after their difficult journey,
while you so easily will wipe away their tears.
At this they weep the more,
yet even their laments are matter for joy,
because you, Lord,
are not some human being of flesh and blood,
but the Lord who made them,
and now make them anew and comfort them.

(V, 2, 2)

You did not let go of my soul

Thanks to your hidden providence, O my God,
your hands did not let go of my soul.
Through my mother's tears
the sacrifice of her heart's blood
was being offered to you day after day,
night after night,
for my welfare;
and you dealt with me in wondrous ways.
You, my God, you it was who dealt so with me;
for *our steps are directed by the Lord,*
and our way is of his choosing.
What other provision is there for our salvation,
but your hand that remakes what you have made?

(V, 7, 13)

I lied to my mother,
my incomparable mother!
But I went free,
because in your mercy you forgave me.
Full of detestable filth as I was,
you kept me safe from the waters of the sea
to bring me to the water of your grace;
once I was washed in that,
the rivers of tears
that flowed from my mother's eyes
would be dried up,
those tears with which day by day
she bedewed the ground
wherever she prayed to you for me.

(V, 8, 15)

Where were you when I sought you?

O you who have been my hope since my youth,
where were you when I sought you?
How was it that you had gone so far away?
Had you not created me
and marked me out *from the four-footed beasts,*
and made me wiser than the birds in the sky?
Yet I was walking a dark and slippery path,
searching for you outside myself
and failing to find the God of my own heart.
I had sunk to the depth of the sea,
I lost all faith
and despaired of ever finding the truth.

(VI, 1, 1)

O God, most high, most deep,
and yet nearer than all else,
most hidden yet intimately present,
you are not framed of greater and lesser limbs;
you are everywhere, whole and entire in every place,
but confined to none.
In no sense is our bodily form to be attributed to you,
yet you have made us in your own image,
and lo! here we are, from head to foot set in our place!

(VI, 3, 4)

I sighed and you heard me

All the while, Lord,
as I pondered these things
you stood by me;
I sighed and you heard me;
I was tossed to and fro
and you steered me aright.
I wandered down the wide road of the world,
but you did not desert me.

(VI, 5, 8)

I put off being converted

I put off being *converted to the Lord*
and from day to day pushed away from me
the day when I would live in you,
though I could not postpone a daily dying in myself.
Though I was so enamored of a happy life
I feared to find it in its true home,
and fled from it even as I sought it.
For I thought I would be exceedingly miserable
if deprived of a woman's embrace,
and gave no thought to the medicine
prepared by your mercy for the healing of this infirmity,
since I had no experience of it
and believed that continence must be achieved
by one's own strength,
a strength of which I was not conscious in my own case.
I was too stupid to realize that, as scripture testifies,
no one can be continent except by your gift.
Yet you would certainly have given me the gift
if I had beaten upon your ears with my inward groans
and cast my care upon you with resolute faith.

(VI, 11, 20)

God will carry us

Oh, how tortuous were those paths!
Woe betide the soul
which supposes it will find something better
if it forsakes you!
Toss and turn as we may,
now on our back, now side, now belly—
our bed is hard at every point,
for you alone are our rest.
But lo! Here you are;
you rescue us from our wretched meanderings
and establish us on your way;
you console us and bid us,
"Run: I will carry you,
I will lead you
and I will bring you home."

(VI, 16, 26)

I searched outside of myself

What agonizing birth-pangs tore my heart,
what groans it uttered, O my God!
And there, unknown to me,
were your hearkening ears,
for as I labored hard in my silent search
the mute sufferings of my mind
reached your mercy as loud cries.
You alone knew my pain, no one else;
for how little of it
could I express in words to my closest friends!
Could their ears have caught all the tumult
that raged in my soul,
when even I had neither time enough
nor eloquence to articulate it?
Yet even as my heart roared its anguish
my clamor found its way to your hearing,
and all my longing lay before you,
for the light of my eyes
was not there at my command:
it was within,
but I was outside;
it occupied no place,
but I had fixed my gaze on spatially positioned things,
and so I found in them nowhere to rest.

(VII, 7, 11)

Praise be to you,
glory be to you,
O fount of all mercy!
As I grew more and more miserable,
you were drawing nearer.
Already your right hand was ready to seize me
and pull me out of the filth,
yet I did not know it.
The only thing that restrained me
from being sucked still deeper
into the whirlpool of carnal lusts
was the fear of death and of your future judgment,
which throughout all the swings of opinion
had never been dislodged from my heart.

(VI, 16, 26)

You gave new form to my deformity

You, Lord, abide for ever
and will not for ever be angry with us,
for you have taken pity on us
who are earth and ashes;
and so it was pleasing in your sight
to give new form to my deformity.
You goaded me within
to make me chafe impatiently
until you should grow clear to my spiritual sight.
At the unseen touch of your medicine
my swelling subsided,
while under the stinging eye-salve of curative pain
the fretful, darkened vision of my spirit
began to improve day by day.

(VII, 8, 12)

In the following prayers
Augustine looks at the itinerary of his conversion
and the birth-pangs that went with it.
But God was with him in this struggle,
and so too, in our daily conversion,
God is with us.

A gradual change

O eternal Truth, true Love, and beloved Eternity,
you are my God,
and for you I sigh day and night.
As I first began to know you
you lifted me up
and showed me
that while that which I might see exists indeed,
I was not yet capable of seeing it.
Your rays beamed intensely upon me,
beating back my feeble gaze,
and I trembled with love and dread.
I knew myself to be far away from you
in a region of unlikeness,
and I seemed to hear your voice from on high:
"I am the food of the mature;
grow then, and you will eat me.
You will not change me into yourself like bodily food:
you will be changed into me."

(VII, 10, 16)

I looked for a way
to gain the strength I needed to enjoy you,
but I did not find it
until I embraced the mediator
between God and humankind,
the man Christ Jesus,
who also is God,
supreme over all things
and blessed for ever.
Not yet had I embraced him,
though he called out,
proclaiming, *I am the Way and the Truth and the Life*,
nor had I known him as the food which,
though I was not yet strong enough to eat it,
he had mingled with our flesh;
for the Word became flesh
so that your Wisdom,
through whom you created all things,
might become for us the milk adapted to our infancy.

(VII, 18, 24)

Grasping the humble Jesus

Not yet was I humble enough
to grasp the humble Jesus as my God,
nor did I know what his weakness had to teach.
Your Word, the eternal Truth
who towers above the higher spheres of your creation,
raises up to himself
those creatures who bow before him;
but in these lower regions
he has built himself a humble dwelling from our clay,
and used it to cast down
from their pretentious selves
those who do not bow before him
and to make a bridge to bring them to himself.
He heals their swollen pride
and nourishes their love,
that they may not wander even further away
through self-confidence,
but rather weaken
as they see before their feet
the Godhead grown weak
by sharing our garments of skin,
and wearily fling themselves down upon him,
so that he may arise and lift them up.

(VII, 18, 24)

Y̶ou are just, O Lord;
but we have sinned, and done wrong,
and acted impiously,
and your hand has lain heavy upon us.
With good reason were we assigned to that ancient sinner
who presides over death,
for he had seduced our will
into imitating that perverse will of his
by which he refused to stand fast in your truth.
What is a human wretch to do?
Who will free him from this death-laden body,
if not your grace,
given through Jesus Christ our Lord,
whom you have begotten coeternal with yourself
and created at the beginning of all your works?
In him the ruler of this world found nothing
that deserved death
yet slew him all the same;
and so the record of debt
that stood against us was annulled.

(VII, 21, 27)

In a spirit of thankfulness
let me recall the mercies
you lavished on me, O my God;
to you let me confess them.
May I be flooded with love for you
until my very bones cry out,
Who is like you, O Lord?
Let me offer you a sacrifice of praise,
for you have snapped my bonds.
How you broke them I will relate,
so that all your worshipers
who hear my tale may exclaim,
"Blessed be the Lord,
blessed in heaven and on earth,
for great and wonderful is his name."

(VIII, 1, 1)

Your words were now firmly implanted
in my heart of hearts,
and I was besieged by you on every side.
Concerning your eternal life
I was now quite certain,
though I had but glimpsed it
like a tantalizing reflection in a mirror;
this had been enough to take from me
any lingering doubt
concerning that imperishable substance
from which every other substance derives its being.
What I now longed for
was not greater certainty about you,
but a more steadfast abiding in you.
In my daily life everything seemed to be teetering,
and my heart needed to be cleansed of the old leaven.
I was attracted to the Way,
which is our Savior himself,
but the narrowness of the path daunted me
and I still could not walk in it.

(VIII, 1, 1)

Joy over one returning to you, Lord

O God, who are so good,
what is it in the human heart
that makes us rejoice more intensely
over the salvation of a soul
which is despaired of
but then freed from grave danger
than we would
if there had always been good prospects for it
and its peril slighter?
You too, merciful Father,
yes, even you are more joyful
over one repentant sinner
than over ninety-nine righteous people
who need no repentance.
And we likewise listen with overflowing gladness
when we hear how the shepherd carries back
on exultant shoulders
the sheep that had strayed,
and how the coin is returned to your treasury
as neighbors share the glee
of the woman who found it,
while the joy of your eucharistic assembly
wrings tears from us
when the story is read in your house
of a younger son who *was dead,*
but has come back to life,
was lost but is found.
You express your own joy through ours,
and through the joy of your angels

who are made holy by their holy charity;
for you yourself are ever the same,
and all transient things,
things which cannot abide constantly
in their mode of being,
are known to your unchanging intelligence.

(VIII, 3, 6)

Come, Lord,
arouse us and call us back,
kindle us and seize us,
prove to us how sweet you are
in your burning tenderness;
let us love you and run to you.
Are there not many who return to you
from a deeper, blinder pit than did Victorinus,
many who draw near to you and are illumined
as they welcome the light,
and in welcoming it
receive from you the power to become children of God?
Yet if they are less well known to the populace,
even people who do know them
find less joy in their conversion,
because whenever joy is shared among many,
even the gladness of individuals is increased,
for all are affected by the common enthusiasm
and they catch the flame from one another.

(VIII, 4, 9)

To find my delight in your law
as far as my inmost self was concerned
was of no profit to me
when a different law in my bodily members
was warring against the law of my mind,
imprisoning me under the law of sin
which held sway in my lower self.
For the law of sin is that brute force of habit
whereby the mind is dragged along
and held fast against its will,
and deservedly so because it slipped into the habit willingly.
In my wretched state,
who was there to free me from this death-doomed body,
save your grace through Jesus Christ our Lord?
You set me free from a craving for sexual gratification
which fettered me like a tight-drawn chain,
and from my enslavement to worldly affairs:
I will confess to your name, O Lord,
my helper and redeemer.

(VIII, 5-12—6, 13)

"O Lord, how long?
How long?
Will you be angry for ever?
Do not remember our age-old sins."
For by these I was conscious of being held prisoner.
I uttered cries of misery: "Why must I go on saying,
'Tomorrow . . . tomorrow'?
Why not now?
Why not put an end to my depravity this very hour?"

(VIII, 12, 28)

You burst my bonds

O Lord, I am your servant,
I am your servant and your handmaid's son.
You burst my bonds asunder,
and to you will I offer a sacrifice of praise.
May my heart and tongue give praise to you,
and all my bones cry out their question,
"Who is like you, O Lord?"
Yes, let them ask,
and then do you respond
and say to my soul,
"I am your salvation."

(IX, 1, 1)

You lightened my burden

O Christ Jesus, my helper and redeemer.
How sweet did it suddenly seem to me
to shrug off those sweet frivolities,
and how glad I now was to get rid of them—
I who had been loath to let them go!
For it was you who cast them out from me,
you, our real and all-surpassing sweetness.
You cast them out
and entered yourself to take their place,
you who are lovelier than any pleasure,
though not to flesh and blood,
more lustrous than any light,
yet more inward than any secret intimacy,
loftier than all honor,
yet not to those who look for loftiness in themselves.
My mind was free at last
from the gnawing need
to seek advancement and riches,
to welter in filth and scratch my itching lust.
Childlike, I chattered away to you,
my glory, my wealth, my salvation,
and my Lord and God.

(IX, 1, 1)

The example of others

With the arrows of your charity
you had pierced our hearts,
and we bore your words within us
like a sword penetrating us to the core.
The examples of your servants,
whom you had changed from murky to luminous beings,
from dead to living men,
were crowding in upon our thoughts,
where they burned and consumed the heavy torpor
that might have pulled us down again.
So powerfully did they ignite us
that every breath of guileful opposition
blew our flame into fiercer heat,
rather than extinguishing us.

(IX, 2, 3)

How loudly I cried out to you, my God,
as I read the psalms of David,
songs full of faith,
outbursts of devotion
with no room in them for the breath of pride!
How loudly I began to cry out to you in those psalms,
how I was inflamed by them with love for you
and fired to recite them to the whole world, were I able,
as a remedy against human pride!
Yet in truth they are sung throughout the world,
and no one can hide from your burning heat.

(IX, 4, 8)

My memory harks back
to our sojourn at Cassiciacum,
and it is my delight, Lord,
to acknowledge before you
what inward goads you employed to tame me,
how you laid low the mountains and hills
of my proud intellect
and made of me an even plain,
how you straightened my winding ways
and smoothed my rugged patches,
and how you also brought my heart's brother, Alypius,
to submit to the name of your only-begotten Son,
our Lord and Savior Jesus Christ.

(IX, 4, 7)

My confession before many witnesses

Let me know you, O you who know me;
then shall I know even as I am known.
You are the strength of my soul;
make your way in and shape it to yourself,
that it may be yours to have and to hold,
free from stain or wrinkle.
I speak because this is my hope,
and whenever my joy springs from that hope
it is joy well founded.
As for the rest of this life's experiences,
the more tears are shed over them
the less are they worth weeping over,
and the more truly worth lamenting
the less do we bewail them while mired in them.
You love the truth
because anyone who "does truth"
comes to the light.
Truth it is that I want to do
in my heart by confession in your presence
and with my pen before many witnesses.

(X, 1, 1)

My confessions are for my neighbor

All the same, my inward healer,
make clear to me what advantage
there is in doing this.
When the confession of my past evil deeds
is read and listened to—
those evil deeds
which you have forgiven and covered over
to make me glad in yourself,
transforming my soul by faith and your sacrament—
that recital arouses the hearer's heart,
forbidding it to slump into despair and say, "I can't."
Let it rather keep watch for your loving mercy
and your gentle grace,
through which every weak soul
that knows its own weakness grows strong.
It is cheering to good people
to hear about the past evil deeds
of those who are now freed from them:
cheering not because the deeds were evil
but because they existed once but exist no more.

(X, 3, 4)

The words of my soul

To you, Lord, I lie exposed,
exactly as I am.
I have spoken of what I hope to gain
by confessing to you.
My confession to you is made
not with words of tongue and voice,
but with the words of my soul
and the clamor of my thought,
to which your ear is attuned;
for when I am bad,
confession to you is simply disgust with myself,
but when I am good,
confession to you consists in
not attributing my goodness to myself,
because though you, Lord, bless the person who is just,
it is only because you first made him just
when he was sinful.
This is why, O my God,
my confession in your presence is silent,
yet not altogether silent:
there is no noise to it, but it shouts by love.
I can say nothing right to other people
unless you have heard it from me first,
nor can you even hear anything of the kind from me
which you have not first told me.

(X, 2, 2)

Our hope is that,
because you are trustworthy,
you do not allow us to be tempted more fiercely
than we can bear,
but along with the temptation
you ordain the outcome of it,
so that we can endure.
Let me, then, confess what I know about myself,
and confess too what I do not know,
because what I know of myself
I know only because you shed light on me,
and what I do not know
I shall remain ignorant about
until my darkness becomes like bright noon
before your face.

(X, 5, 7)

It is no small gain,
O Lord my God,
if thanks are offered to you by many people
on our account
and many pray to you for us.
Yes, let a brotherly mind love in me
what you teach us to be worthy of love,
and deplore in me what you teach us to be deplorable.
But let it be a brotherly mind that does this,
not the mind of a stranger,
not the minds of alien foes
who mouth falsehood
and whose power wreaks wickedness;
let it be a brotherly mind
which when it approves of me will rejoice over me,
and when it disapproves
will be saddened on my account,
because whether it approves or disapproves
it still loves me.
To such people I will disclose myself:
let them sigh with relief over my good actions,
but with grief over my evil deeds.
The good derive from you and are your gift;
the evil are my sins and your punishments.
Let them sigh with relief over the one
and with grief over the other,
and let both hymns and laments
ascend into your presence

from the hearts of my brethren,
which are your censers.
And then do you, Lord, in your delight
at the fragrance which pervades your holy temple,
have mercy on me according to your great mercy
for the sake of your name.
Do not, I entreat you,
do not abandon your unfinished work,
but bring to perfection
all that is wanting in me.

(X, 4, 5)

My people, let me be heard

When I confess not what I have been
but what I am now,
this is the fruit to be reaped from my confessions:
I confess not only before you in secret exultation
tinged with fear
and secret sorrow infused with hope,
but also in the ears of believing men and women,
the companions of my joy
and sharers in my mortality,
my fellow citizens still on pilgrimage with me,
those who have gone before
and those who will follow,
and all who bear me company in my life.
They are your servants and my brethren,
but you have willed them to be your children
and my masters,
and you have ordered me to serve them
if I wish to live with you and share your life.
This command of yours would mean little to me
if it were only spoken,
and not first carried out in deed as well.
So I do likewise,
and I do it in deeds and in words;
I do it under your outstretched wings,
and would do it in grave peril,
were it not that under those wings
my soul is surrendered to you
and to you my weakness known.
I am a little child,

but my Father lives for ever
and in him I have a guardian suited to me.
He who begot me is also he who keeps me safe;
you yourself are all the good I have,
you are almighty
and you are with me before ever I am with you.
To such people, then,
the people you command me to serve,
I will disclose myself not as I have been
but as I am now, as I am still,
though I do not judge myself.
In this way, then, let me be heard.

(X, 4, 6)

It is you, Lord, who judge me.
No one knows what he himself is made of,
except his own spirit within him,
yet there is still some part of him
which remains hidden even from his own spirit;
but you, Lord, know everything about a human being
because you have made him.
And though in your sight
I may despise myself and reckon myself dust and ashes
I know something about you
which I do not know about myself.
It is true that we now see
only a tantalizing reflection in a mirror,
and so it is that while I am on pilgrimage far from you
I am more present to myself than to you;
yet I do know
that you cannot be defiled in any way whatever,
whereas I do not know which temptations
I may have the strength to resist,
and to which ones I shall succumb.

(X, 5, 7)

I love you, Lord,
with no doubtful mind
but with absolute certainty.
You pierced my heart with your word,
and I fell in love with you.
But the sky and the earth too,
and everything in them—
all these things around me
are telling me that I should love you;
and since they never cease to proclaim this to everyone,
those who do not hear are left without excuse.
But you, far above, will show mercy
to anyone with whom you have already determined
to deal mercifully,
and will grant pity to whomsoever you choose.
Were this not so,
the sky and the earth would be proclaiming
your praises to the deaf.

(X, 6, 8)

This is what I love, when I love my God

What am I loving when I love you?
Not beauty of body nor transient grace,
not this fair light
which is now so friendly to my eyes,
not melodious song in all its lovely harmonies,
not the sweet fragrance of flowers or ointments or spices,
not manna or honey,
not limbs that draw me to carnal embrace:
none of these do I love when I love my God.
And yet I do love a kind of light,
a kind of voice, a certain fragrance,
a food and an embrace,
when I love my God:
a light, voice, fragrance,
food and embrace for my inmost self,
where something limited to no place shines into my mind,
where something not snatched away
by passing time sings for me,
where something no breath blows away
yields to me its scent,
where there is savor undiminished by famished eating,
and where I am clasped
in a union from which no satiety can tear me away.
This is what I love, when I love my God.

(X, 6, 8)

Augustine now gives praise to God
for the gift of memory.
He shows how memory is a beautiful part of life,
and that through it we can recall
the wonderful aspects of the past and present,
especially the constant love of God in our lives and struggles.
We too need to recognize and appreciate this gift of memory.

The faculty of memory

This faculty of memory is a great one, O my God,
exceedingly great, a vast, infinite recess.
Who can plumb its depth?
This is a faculty of my mind,
belonging to my nature,
yet I cannot myself comprehend all that I am.
Is the mind, then, too narrow to grasp itself,
forcing us to ask where that part of it is
which it is incapable of grasping?
Is it outside the mind, not inside?
How can the mind not compass it?
Enormous wonder wells up within me
when I think of this, and I am dumbfounded.

(X, 8, 15)

I never forgot you, Lord

From that time when I learned about you
I have never forgotten you,
because wherever I have found truth
I have found my God who is absolute Truth,
and once I had learned that I did not forget it.
That is why you have dwelt in my memory
ever since I learned to know you,
and it is there that I find you
when I remember and delight in you.
These are my holy delights,
and they are your gift to me,
for in your mercy
you look graciously upon my poverty.

(X, 24, 35)

How awesome a mystery is memory

O my God, profound, infinite complexity,
what a great faculty memory is,
how awesome a mystery!
It is the mind,
and this is nothing other than my very self.
What am I, then, O my God?
What is my nature?
It is teeming life of every conceivable kind,
and exceedingly vast.
See, in the measureless plains and vaults
and caves of my memory,
immeasurably full of countless kinds of things
which are there either through their images
(as with material things),
or by being themselves present
(as is the knowledge acquired
through a liberal education),
or by registering themselves
and making their mark in some indefinable way
(as with emotional states
which the memory retains
even when the mind is not actually experiencing them,
although whatever is in the memory
must be in the mind too)—
in this wide land I am made free of all of them,
free to run and fly to and fro,
to penetrate as deeply as I can,
to collide with no boundary anywhere.
So great is the faculty of memory,

so great the power of life in a person
whose life is tending toward death!

(X, 17, 26)

How shall I find you?

What shall I do then, O my God, my true life?
I will pass beyond this faculty of mine called memory,
I will pass beyond it
and continue resolutely toward you, O lovely Light.
What are you saying to me?
See, I am climbing through my mind to you
who abide high above me;
I will pass beyond even this faculty of mine
which is called memory
in my longing to touch you from that side
whence you can be touched,
and cleave to you
in the way in which holding fast to you is possible.
For animals and birds also have memories;
they would not otherwise return
to their accustomed lairs and nests,
rather than randomly to others,
and indeed they would never be able
to grow accustomed to anything without memory.
I will therefore pass beyond memory
and try to touch him
who marked me out from the four-footed beasts
and made me wiser than the birds in the sky;
yes, I will pass beyond even my memory
that I may find you . . . where?
O my true good,
O sweetness that will never fail me,
that I may find you . . . where?
If I find you somewhere beyond my memory,

that means that I shall be forgetful of you.
And how shall I find you,
once I am no longer mindful of you?

(X, 17, 26)

O Truth,
you hold sovereign sway over all
who turn to you for counsel,
and to all of them you respond at the same time,
however diverse their pleas.
Clear is your response,
but not all hear it clearly.
They all appeal to you about what they want,
but do not always hear what they want to hear.
Your best servant is the one
who is less intent on hearing from you
what accords with his own will,
and more on embracing with his will
what he has heard from you.

(X, 26, 37)

Late, have I loved you!

Late have I loved you, Beauty so ancient and so new,
late have I loved you!
Lo, you were within, but I outside,
seeking there for you,
and upon the shapely things you have made
I rushed headlong,
I, misshapen.
You were with me, but I was not with you.
They held me back far from you,
those things which would have no being
were they not in you.
You called, shouted, broke through my deafness;
you flared, blazed, banished my blindness;
you lavished your fragrance,
I gasped, and now I pant for you;
I tasted you, and I hunger and thirst;
you touched me, and I burned for your peace.

(X, 27, 38)

You are the physician; I am sick

When at last I cling to you with my whole being
there will be no more anguish or labor for me,
and my life will be alive indeed,
because filled with you.
But now it is very different.
Anyone whom you fill you also uplift,
but I am not full of you,
and so I am a burden to myself.
Joys over which I ought to weep
do battle with sorrows
that should be matter for joy,
and I know not which will be victorious.
But I also see griefs that are evil at war in me
with joys that are good,
and I know not which will win the day.
This is agony, Lord, have pity on me!
It is agony!
See, I do not hide my wounds;
you are the physician and I am sick;
you are merciful, I in need of mercy.
Is not human life on earth a time of testing?

(X, 28, 39)

A time of testing

Who would choose troubles and hardships?
You command us to endure them,
but not to love them.
No one loves what he has to endure,
even if he loves the endurance,
for although he may rejoice in his power to endure,
he would prefer to have nothing
that demands endurance.
In adverse circumstances I long for prosperity,
and in times of prosperity I dread adversity.
What middle ground is there between the two,
where human life might be free from trial?
Woe and woe again betide worldly prosperity,
from fear of disaster and evanescent joy!
But woe, woe, and woe again upon worldly adversity,
from envy of better fortune,
the hardship of adversity itself,
and the fear that endurance may falter.
Is not human life on earth
a time of testing without respite?

(X, 28, 39)

Dust we are, Lord,
and remember that from this dust
you made us,
and that our race, once lost,
was found again.
Strengthen me, that I may be capable,
give what you command,
and then command whatever you will.
O holy God, my God,
when what you command is done,
it is by your gift.

(X, 31, 45)

You reveal me, Lord

You are Truth,
and in you I see that if I am touched
by the high opinion others hold of me,
it should be not for my own sake
but so that my neighbor may profit thereby.
And whether this is the case,
I do not know.
In this respect
I know myself less clearly than I know you.
I beg you to reveal myself to me as well, O my God,
so that I may confess the wounded condition
I diagnose in myself to my brethren,
who will pray for me.

(X, 37, 62)

O my God, for me you are loveliness itself;
yet for all these things too
I sing a hymn and offer a sacrifice of praise
to you who sanctify me,
because the beautiful designs
that are born in our minds
and find expression through clever hands
derive from that Beauty which transcends all minds,
the Beauty to which my own mind aspires day and night.
Those who create beauty in material things,
and those who seek it,
draw from that source their power to appreciate beauty,
but not the norm for its use.
The norm is there,
and could they but see it
they would need to search no further.
They could save their strength for you
rather than dissipate it on enervating luxuries.
As for me,
I say all these things and recognize their truth,
yet still I snag my steps on these beautiful objects;
but you pluck me free, Lord,
you pluck me free
because my eyes are fixed on your mercy.
I am miserably caught,
but you mercifully extricate me,
sometimes without my being aware of it,
when I am only lightly entangled,
but sometimes painfully
because I am already stuck fast.

(X, 34, 53)

Needy and poor am I,
but I am the better for recognizing it
and lamenting it in secret,
and seeking your mercy
until my shortcomings are made good
and my imperfect self
brought to perfection in a peace
which the gaze of the arrogant
will never descry.
But words proceed from the mouth,
and actions are observed by other people,
and this is fraught with peril,
because a hankering for praise
will garner every little tribute of approval
it can beg,
to bolster some fancied preeminence of its own.
This is a real temptation to me,
and even when I am accusing myself of it,
the very fact that I am accusing myself
tempts me to further self-esteem.
We can make our very contempt for vainglory
a ground for preening ourselves more vainly still,
which proves that
what we are congratulating ourselves on
is certainly not contempt for vainglory;
for no one who indulges in it can be despising it.

(X, 38, 63)

Summary of all my discoveries

O Truth,
is there any road
where you have not walked with me,
teaching me what to avoid and what to aim at,
whenever I referred to you
the paltry insights I had managed to attain,
and sought your guidance?
I surveyed the external world as best I could
with the aid of my senses,
and studied the life
my body derives from my spirit,
and my senses themselves.
Then I moved inward to the storehouse of my memory,
to those vast, complex places
amazingly filled with riches beyond counting;
I contemplated them and was adread.
No single one of them
could I have perceived without you,
but I found that no single one of them was you.
But what of myself, the discoverer,
I who scanned them all
and tried to distinguish them
and evaluate each in accordance with its proper dignity?
Some things I questioned as my senses reported them,
others I felt to be inextricably part of myself;
I classified and counted the very messengers,
and in the ample stores of memory
I scrutinized some items,
pushed some into the background

and dragged others into the light:
what, then of me?
No, I was not you, either,
not even I as I did all this:
the faculty, that is, by which I achieved it,
not even that faculty in me was you;
for you are that abiding Light
whom I consulted throughout my search.
I questioned you about each thing,
asking whether it existed,
what it was,
how highly it should be regarded;
and all the while I listened to you teaching me
and laying your commands upon me.

(X, 40, 65)

Christk Jesus the mediator

In your unfathomable mercy
you first gave the humble
certain pointers to the true Mediator,
and then sent him,
that by his example
they might learn even a humility like his.
This Mediator between God and humankind,
the man Christ Jesus,
appeared to stand between mortal sinners
and the God who is immortal and just:
like us he was mortal,
but like God he was just.
Now the wage due to justice is life and peace;
and so through the justice
whereby he was one with God
he broke the power of death
on behalf of malefactors rendered just,
using that very death
to which he willed to be liable along with them.
He was pointed out to holy people
under the old dispensation
that they might be saved
through faith in his future passion,
as we are through faith in that passion
now accomplished.
Only in virtue of his humanity is he the Mediator;
in his nature as the Word
he does not stand between us and God,
for he is God's equal, God with God,
and with him one only God.

(X, 43, 68)

You redeemed me, Lord

Lord, I cast my care upon you
that I may live,
and I will contemplate the wonders
you have revealed.
You know how stupid and weak I am:
teach me and heal me.
Your only Son,
in whom are hidden all treasures of wisdom and knowledge,
has redeemed me with his blood.
Let not the proud disparage me,
for I am mindful of my ransom.
I eat it, I drink it,
I dispense it to others,
and as a poor man I long to be filled with it
among those who are fed and feasted.
And then do those who seek him
praise the Lord.

(X, 43, 70)

Augustine realizes that paramount in his journey
from unquiet restlessness to rest and peace
is his desire for God,
and this dominates the prayers of this section.
He lived his monastic and clerical life
with this constant desire for God
and preached it and portrayed it in his writings.
We too have a desire for God and must cultivate and enrich it.

Our hope is that
we may cease to be miserable in ourselves
and may find our beatitude in you;
for you have called us to be poor in spirit,
to be meek, to mourn,
to hunger and thirst for righteousness,
to be merciful and pure-hearted,
and to be peacemakers.

(XI, 1, 1)

Eternity belongs to you, O Lord,
so surely you can neither be ignorant
of what I am telling you
nor view what happens in time
as though you were conditioned by time yourself?
Why then am I relating all this to you at such length?
Certainly not in order to inform you.
I do it to arouse my own loving devotion toward you,
and that of my readers,
so that together we may declare,
Great is the Lord, and exceedingly worthy of praise.
I have said already, and will say again,
that it is out of love for loving you
that I do this,
even as we pray for things
though Truth tells us
that *Your Father knows what you need before you ask him.*
We confess to you our miseries
and the mercies you have shown us
in your will to set us free completely,
as you have begun to do already;
and by so confessing to you
we lay bare our loving devotion.

(XI, 1, 1)

Hearken, O Lord, have mercy,
my Lord and God,
O Light of the blind, Strength of the weak —
who yet are Light to those who see
and Strength to the strong —
hearken to my soul,
hear me as I cry from the depths,
for unless your ears be present in our deepest places
where shall we go and whither cry?
Yours is the day, yours the night,
a sign from you sends minutes speeding by;
spare in their fleeting course a space for us
to ponder the hidden wonders of your law:
shut it not against us as we knock.

(XI, 2, 3)

Let me open up to you, Lord

Not in vain do harts and hinds seek shelter in the woods,
to hide and venture forth,
roam and browse, lie down and ruminate.
Perfect me too, Lord, and reveal those woods to me.
Lo, your voice is joy to me,
your voice that rings out above a flood of joys.
Give me what I love;
for I love indeed, and this love you have given me.
Forsake not your gifts, disdain not your parched grass.
Let me confess to you all I have found in your books.
Let me hear the voice of praise,
and drink from you,
and contemplate the wonders of your law
from the beginning when you made heaven and earth
to that everlasting reign
when we shall be with you in your holy city.

(XI, 2, 3)

O Lord my God, hear my prayer,
may your mercy hearken to my longing,
a longing on fire not for myself alone
but to serve the brethren I dearly love;
you see my heart and know this is true.
Let me offer in sacrifice to you
the service of my heart and tongue,
but grant me first what I can offer you;
for I am needy and poor,
but you are rich unto all who call upon you,
and you care for us
though no care troubles you.
Circumcise all that is within me from presumption
and my lips without from falsehood.
Let your scriptures be my chaste delight,
let me not be deceived in them
nor through them deceive others.

(XI, 2, 3)

Have mercy on me, Lord,
and hearken to my longing;
for I do not think it arises from this earth,
or concerns itself with gold or silver or precious stones,
with splendid raiment or honors or positions of power,
with the pleasures of the flesh
or with things we need for the body
and for this our life of pilgrimage;
for all these things are provided
for those who seek your kingdom
and your righteousness.
Look and see, O my God, whence springs my desire.
The unrighteous have told me titillating tales,
but they have nothing to do with your law, O Lord;
and see, that law is what stirs my longing.
See, Father, have regard to me
and see and bless my longing,
and let it be pleasing in your merciful eyes
that I find grace before you,
so that the inner meaning of your words
may be opened to me
as I knock at their door.
I beg this grace through our Lord Jesus Christ, your Son,
the man at your right hand,
the Son of Man
whom you have made strong
to stand between yourself and us as mediator.

(XI, 2, 4)

You seek me, Lord

Through Jesus you sought us
when we were not seeking you,
but you sought us that we might begin to seek you.
He is the Word through whom you made all things,
and me among them,
your only Son
through whom you called your believing people
to be your sons by adoption,
and me among them;
through him, then, do I make my plea to you,
through him who sits at your right hand to intercede for us,
for in him are hidden all treasures
of wisdom and knowledge.

(XI, 2, 4)

Let everyone who has the aptitude
listen to your spoken word within;
for my part I will begin with confidence
from your word in scripture, and cry out,
How magnificent are your works, O Lord!
In wisdom you have created all things.
This wisdom is no other than the Beginning,
and in that Beginning you have made heaven and earth.

(XI, 9, 11)

What is this light
that shines through the chinks of my mind
and pierces my heart, doing it no injury?
I begin to shudder yet catch fire with longing:
I shudder inasmuch as I am unlike him,
yet I am afire with longing for him
because some likeness there is.
Wisdom it is, none other than Wisdom,
that shines through my darkness,
tearing apart the cloud that envelops me;
yet I fall away from it
and am plunged into obscurity once more,
lost in the murk and rubble that are my punishment,
for so wasted away is my strength
to the point of destitution
that I cannot even support the good that I have,
until you, O Lord,
who are mercifully disposed toward all my sins,
heal all my ailments too.
And I know you will,
for you will rescue my life from decay,
crown me in pity and mercy,
and overwhelmingly satisfy my desire with good things;
and my youth will be renewed like an eagle's.

(XI, 9, 11)

Help me to understand

Give me what I love;
for I love indeed,
and this love you have given me.
Give this to me, Father,
for you truly know how to give good gifts to your children;
Give me this gift,
for I have only just begun to understand,
and the labor is too much for me
until you open the door.
Through Christ I implore you,
in the name of that holy of holies,
let no noisy person stand in my way.
I too have believed,
and so I too speak.
This is my hope,
for this I live:
to contemplate the delight of the Lord.
See how old you have made my days;
they are slipping away and I know not how.

(XI, 22, 28)

My lowly tongue lauds your sublime majesty,
for you have made heaven and earth:
this heaven which I see,
and the earth on which I tread,
and this frame of clay I carry—you made them all.
But where, Lord, is that *heaven's heaven*
of which we hear in the psalm:
Heaven's heaven is for the Lord;
but he has assigned the earth to humankind?
Where is that heaven we cannot see,
in comparison with which all we can see is but earth?
This whole material world has been endowed
with beauty of form even in its furthest parts,
the lowest of which is our earth;
yet compared with *heaven's heaven*
the heaven that overarches our earth
is itself no better than earth.
And not without good reason are those two vast realities
—our earth and our sky—
to be regarded as mere lowly earth
beside that unimaginable heaven
which is for the Lord, not for humankind.

(XII, 2, 2)

O Truth, illumination of my heart,
let not my own darkness speak to me!
I slid away to material things, sank into shadow,
yet even there, even from there, I loved you.
Away I wandered, yet I remembered you.
I heard your voice behind me, calling me back,
yet scarcely heard it for the tumult of the unquiet.
See now, I come back to you,
fevered and panting for your fountain.
Let no one bar my way,
let me drink it and draw life from it.
Let me not be my own life:
evil was the life I lived of myself;
I was death to me; but in you I begin to live again.
Speak to me yourself, converse with me.
I have believed your scriptures,
but those words are full of hidden meaning.

(XII, 10, 10)

Loud and clear have you spoken to me already
in my inward ear, O Lord,
telling me that you are eternal,
and to you alone immortality belongs,
because no alteration of form,
no motion, changes you.
Nor does your will vary with changing times,
for a will that can be sometimes one thing,
sometimes another, is not immortal.
In your sight this is clear to me,
but I beg you that it may grow clearer still,
and in that disclosure I will prudently stand firm
beneath your wings.

(XII, 11, 11)

You, O God,
show yourself to anyone who loves you
according to your bidding,
and are wholly sufficient to him,
so that such a one turns not aside from you or to himself.
This order of creation is God's house,
neither terrestrial nor some massive celestial building,
but a spiritual structure which shares your eternity,
and is unstained for ever.
You have established it to last for ever,
and your ordinance will not pass away.
Yet it is not coeternal with you,
for it did have a beginning: it was created.

(XII, 15, 19)

You carry me

O lightsome house, so fair of form,
I have fallen in love with your beauty,
loved you as the place where dwells the glory of my Lord,
who fashioned you and claims you as his own.
My pilgrim-soul sighs for you,
and I pray him who made you to claim me also
as his own within you, for he made me too.
Like a lost sheep I have gone astray,
but on the shoulders of my shepherd, your builder,
I hope to be carried back to you.

(XII, 15, 21)

Your goodness was with me

You have blotted out all the evils in me
that deserved your punishment, Lord,
not requiting me for the work of my hands,
by which I defected from you to my own unmaking,
and you have anticipated all my good actions,
rewarding the work of your own hands that made me;
for before ever I was, you were;
I did not even exist to receive your gift of being;
yet lo! now I do exist, thanks to your goodness.
Over all that I am,
both what you have made me
and that from which you made me,
your goodness has absolute precedence.
You had no need of me.
You command me to serve you and worship you
that it may be well with me of your bounty,
who have granted me first to exist,
that I may enjoy well-being.

(XIII, 1, 1)

You never forget me, Lord

Upon you I call, O God, my mercy,
who made me and did not forget me
when I forgot you.
Into my soul I call you,
for you prepare it to be your dwelling
by the desire you inspire in it.
Do not forsake me now when I call upon you,
who before ever I called on you forestalled me
by your persistent, urgent entreaties,
multiplying and varying your appeals
that I might hear you from afar,
and turn back,
and begin to call upon you
who were calling me.

(XIII, 1, 1)

Your spirit gives us rest

In your Gift we find rest,
and there we enjoy you.
Our true place is where we find rest.
We are borne toward it by love,
and it is your good Spirit
who lifts up our sunken nature
from the gates of death.
In goodness of will is our peace.
A body gravitates to its proper place
by its own weight.
This weight does not necessarily drag it downward,
but pulls it to the place proper to it:
thus fire tends upward, a stone downward.
Drawn by their weight,
things seek their rightful places.
If oil is poured into water,
it will rise to the surface,
but if water is poured onto oil
it will sink below the oil.
Drawn by their weight,
things seek their rightful places.
They are not at rest
as long as they are disordered,
but once brought to order they find their rest.
Now, my weight is my love,
and wherever I am carried,
it is this weight that carries me.
Your Gift sets us afire
and we are borne upward;

we catch his flame and up we go.
In our hearts we climb those upward paths,
singing the songs of ascent.
By your fire, your beneficent fire,
are we enflamed,
because we are making our way up
to *the peace of Jerusalem.*
For *I rejoiced when I was told,*
"We are going to the Lord's house."
There shall a good will find us a place,
that we may have no other desire
but to abide there for ever.

(XIII, 9, 10)

Give me yourself, O my God,
give yourself back to me.
Lo, I love you,
but if my love is too mean,
let me love more passionately.
I cannot gauge my love,
nor know how far it fails,
how much more love I need for my life
to set its course straight into your arms,
never swerving until hidden in the covert of your face.
This alone I know,
that without you all to me is misery,
woe outside myself and woe within,
and all wealth but penury,
if it is not my God.

(XIII, 8, 9)

My God

In the morning
I will stand and see my God,
who sheds the light of salvation on my face,
who will breathe life even into our mortal bodies
through the Spirit who dwells in us
and has been mercifully hovering over
the dark chaos of our inner being.
By this we have received,
even on our pilgrim way,
the pledge that we are children of the light already.
Saved only in hope we may be,
but we are at home in the light and in the day.
No longer are we children of the night or of darkness,
as once we were.
But you alone distinguish between us and the night-born
in this present uncertainty
where human knowledge falters,
for you test our hearts
and call light "day" and darkness "night."
Who but you can tell them apart?
Yet what do we possess
that we have not received from you,
since from the one same lump
you have formed us for honorable service,
and others for common use?

(XIII, 14, 15)

Let us contemplate the heavens,
the work of your fingers, O Lord;
clear away that cloud
you have spread beneath them,
hiding them from our eyes.
There is the witness you have borne to yourself,
and to little ones it imparts wisdom.
Out of the mouths of infants and sucklings
evoke perfect praise, O my God.
We know no other books with the like power
to lay pride low
and so surely to silence the obstinate contender
who tries to thwart your reconciling work
by defending his sins.
Nowhere else, Lord,
indeed nowhere else
do I know such chaste words,
words with such efficacy
to persuade me to confession,
to gentle my neck beneath your kindly yoke
and invite me to worship you without thought of reward.
Grant me understanding of your words, good Father,
give me this gift,
stationed as I am below them,
because it is for us earth-dwellers
that you have fashioned that strong vault overhead.

(XIII, 15, 17)

The vision of you as you are

Clouds are wafted away, but heaven abides.
Preachers of your word are wafted away
out of this life into another,
but your scripture remains
stretched above your people everywhere
until the end of the world.
Then will even sky and earth be swept away,
but your utterances will stand unmoved,
because though the tent is folded
and the grass where it was pitched
withers with all its verdure,
your Word abides for ever.
Not as he is, but tantalizingly,
as though veiled by cloud and mirrored in his heaven,
does this Word appear to us now,
for though we are the beloved of your Son,
it has not yet appeared what we shall be.
He peeps through the trellis of our flesh,
and coaxes us,
and enkindles our love until we run after him,
allured by his fragrance.
But when he appears, we shall be like him,
because we shall see him as he is.
Our seeing then, Lord,
will be the vision of you as you are,
but this is not granted to us yet.

(XIII, 15, 18)

I pray you, Lord:
as you cause joy and strength to spring up and grow,
even so let the truth spring up:
let it sprout from the earth,
and let righteousness look down from heaven
and let luminaries be set in the firmament.
Let us break our bread for the hungry
and bring the homeless poor under our roof,
let us clothe the naked and not spurn our own kin.
When these fruits are burgeoning on earth,
take heed and see that it is good.
Then may swift dawn break for us,
so that rising from this lowly crop of active works
to the delights of contemplation,
we may lay hold on the Word of Life above,
and appear like luminaries for the world,
firmly set in the vault that is your scripture.
There you school us to mark the distinction
between realities of the mind and sensible things,
as between day and night,
or between souls devoted to the life of the mind
and others preoccupied with sensible matters.

(XIII, 18, 22)

No longer is it you alone
who in the secret recesses of your own judgment
separate light from darkness,
as before that vault was made;
for now that your grace is manifested throughout the world
your spiritual children too,
set in the vault and plainly visible,
may shine upon the earth,
separate day from night,
and mark distinct periods of time.
This is because old things have passed away now
and all is made new;
our salvation is nearer now
than when we first believed;
night is far gone and day is breaking.
You crown the year with your blessing,
sending laborers into your harvest
where others have toiled over the sowing.
Different workers you send to sow new crops,
which will be reaped at the end.

(XIII, 18, 22)

The peace of the Sabbath

Give us peace, Lord God,
for you have given us all else;
give us the peace that is repose,
the peace of the Sabbath,
and the peace that knows no evening.
This whole order of exceedingly good things,
intensely beautiful as it is,
will pass away when it has served its purpose:
these things too will have
their morning and their evening.
But the seventh day has no evening
and sinks toward no sunset,
for you sanctified it that it might abide for ever.
After completing your exceedingly good works
you rested on the seventh day,
though you achieved them in repose;
and you willed your book to tell us this
as a promise that when our works are finished
(works exceedingly good
inasmuch as they are your gift to us)
we too may rest in you,
in the Sabbath of eternal life.
And then you will rest in us,
as now you work in us,
and your rest will be rest through us
as now those works of yours are wrought through us.
But you yourself, Lord, are ever working, ever resting.
You neither see for a time
nor change for a time

nor enjoy repose for a time,
yet you create our temporal seeing and time itself
and our repose after time.

(XIII, 35, 50—37, 52)

Your creation sings praise to you
so that we may love you,
and we love you
so that praise may be offered to you by your creation.
Created things have their beginning and their end in time,
their rising and setting,
their growth and decline,
their beauty of form and their formlessness;
and thus they have their morning and evening,
though sometimes this is hidden,
sometimes plainly seen.
All these things we see to be exceedingly good,
because you see them in us,
you who have given us the Spirit
to enable us to see them,
and in them to love you.

(XIII, 33, 48)

CPSIA information can be obtained at www.ICGtesting.com
Printed in the USA
BVOW070651240513

321534BV00001B/3/P